THE GHOSTLY TALES OF PANAMA CITY

Published by Arcadia Children's Books
A Division of Arcadia Publishing
Charleston, SC
www.arcadiapublishing.com

First published 2023

Manufactured in the United States

ISBN 978-1-4671-9742-7

Library of Congress Control Number: 2023937853

Images used courtesy of Shutterstock.com; p. 8 Catherine Cornish/Shutterstock.com; p. 98 Stephanie A Sellers/Shutterstock.com.

Spooky America

THE GHOSTLY TALES OF PANAMA CITY

PATRICIA HEYER

Adapted from Haunted Panama City by Beverly Nield

ALABAMA
GEORGIA
FLORIDA
GULF OF MEXICO

Table of Contents & Map Key

Welcome to Spooky Panama City! 3

1 Chapter 1. A Ghostly Fisherman at Bayou Joe's 9

2 Chapter 2. Ghosts in the Spotlight! 15

3 Chapter 3. The House Where No One Is Welcome 21

4 Chapter 4. Ghostly Specter of the Schooner *Cleopatra* 31

5 Chapter 5. The Family That Adopted a Ghost 37

6 Chapter 6. The Haunted Manor on Grace Avenue. 45

7 Chapter 7. A Ghost With a Mind of Its Own. 51

8 Chapter 8. Ghostly Doubles Mean Double-Trouble 57

9 Chapter 9. Haunted or Not? That Is the Question!. 65

10 Chapter 10. The Lonely Ghost in the Window. 71

11 Chapter 11. Ghosts of the Cove 79

12 Chapter 12. A Haunting on Harrison Avenue 87

13 Chapter 13. Haunted Chairs & Ghostly in Pairs 93

14 Chapter 14. Can a Lighthouse Outrun Its Ghosts? 99

A Ghostly Goodbye 105

Welcome to Spooky Panama City!

For hundreds of years, Panama City, Florida, has been said to host restless spirits and creepy happenings. They can occur anywhere around here, in creepy mansions or even your own backyard! The ghostly visitors of Panama City like to hang out just about anywhere, from government offices and small businesses to the bays and bayous of the Gulf shore.

But these are not your average hauntings. In Panama City, the ghosts have little twists and quirks of their own. Mysterious sightings and shadowy phantoms have been seen all across Panama City for as long as its citizens can remember.

The following are tales of paranormal disturbances, unexplained events, and hauntings from history, pieced together through old-time newspapers and magazine articles. They shock readers with spine-chilling reporting from this region's earliest days, all the way back to when this was the home of Indigenous peoples. The sites of their villages and burial grounds have been found all across Panama City, but that's not all that has been found!

Some tales come from the days of the great sailing ships and the growth of shipbuilding in the Gulf. Other spooky sightings come from the time of the American Revolution, when the indigo plant grown in the South was important to the American patriots. They used it to make medicines, clean wounds, and as a dye for uniforms and paint. Today, we have modern science and other advances in technology to address those needs. But back then, soldiers relied on their skills and whatever was available to them to survive.

Nonetheless, the battles that occurred here during times of war have taken many a soul, and some believe those souls still roam the shoreline of St. Andrews Bay. In fact, the bay and the many bayous that nearly encircle Panama City play host to dozens of hauntings and strange happenings that just cannot be explained. No wonder Panama City is one of the most *haunted* places in all of Florida!

During the dark days of the yellow fever outbreak, tens of thousands died from the deadly disease. In those days, doctors and scientists hadn't yet discovered that mosquitos bites transmit yellow fever, and there was no way to prevent people from catching it. More than thirty years passed before anyone could get a vaccine to protect themselves against the terrible infection. But by then, entire families had gotten sick and died. The people of Panama City suffered great loss as husbands, wives, mothers, fathers, and even children succumbed to yellow fever—and those who managed to stay alive lived in fear of the heinous disease. With so many lives lost and so much heartbreak, is it any surprise their restless souls still haunt the streets and shores of Panama City?

Well, that's hard to say for sure, but here's a bit of advice: when it comes to all things spooky, it's best to hold judgement before hearing all the facts. So, sit back, relax (if you can), and get to know the ghostly inhabitants of Panama City!

FRESH SHRIMP
CAUGHT DAILY
OPEN 7:00 AM - 9:00 AM
850-596-0798

A Ghostly Fisherman at Bayou Joe's

The Massalina Bayou lies in the very heart of Panama City. Although countless homes and businesses line the bayou, one of the most famous is Bayou Joe's Marina & Grill. Rebuilt after the 2018 Hurricane Michael, Bayou Joe's stands on stilts hovering over the water. Tourists and locals sit side by side on the floating dock enjoying fresh local seafood. Afterward, they can hand-feed the catfish or watch the countless forms of bayou wildlife attracted by underwater lighting.

However, what you may not know is there has been a marina and restaurant here since the 1940s. In the early days, the fishermen gathered here to swap stories and mend their fishing nets. The owner, best known as Old Man Etheridge, was popular on the bayou. He helped out local fishermen whenever he could and always seemed to have a bit of candy for children visiting the marina.

The restaurant has changed hands eight times over the years and survived more than a dozen major storms. Today, Bayou Joe's is not only one of the busiest spots along the Panama City waterfront, but it's also one of the most haunted. And by no ordinary ghost.

There have been tales of strange happenings and eerie lights spotted along the waterfront

for many years. There are even rumors of phantom pirates and haunted ships. However, the best-known story is the one told by Chef Kevin, who met the ghostly fisherman late one night. But first, you need to know that Chef Kevin never believed in ghosts—that is, not until he met the fisherman!

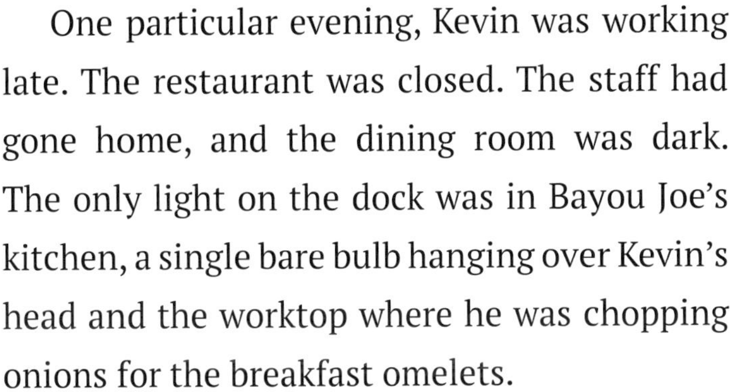

One particular evening, Kevin was working late. The restaurant was closed. The staff had gone home, and the dining room was dark. The only light on the dock was in Bayou Joe's kitchen, a single bare bulb hanging over Kevin's head and the worktop where he was chopping onions for the breakfast omelets.

He was slicing the last onion when he heard the creak of the screen door opening in the dining room. A moment later, there was a loud bang as the door slammed shut. Kevin called out, but there was no answer. He was still holding the twelve-inch chef knife he used to cut the onions as he walked into the darkened dining room. Again, he yelled out.

"*Who's there?*"

But there was no answer. Chef Kevin walked farther into the darkened dining room when something inconceivable caught his attention. Standing near the piling at the edge of the dock was a man in a bright yellow fisherman's slicker staring out across the bayou. Before Kevin could speak, the man in the slicker turned to look at him. It was an old face, gray and wrinkled, yet vibrant enough to be startled.

Then, in an instant, the fisherman vanished!

Kevin couldn't believe his eyes! First, he searched every inch of the restaurant. Grabbing a flashlight, he inspected the parking lot, checked the boat ramps, and even peeked under the canvases of the boats docked in the marina. But he found nothing.

Over time, others also claimed to have seen the mysterious phantom seaman. Once, he was spotted near the entrance to the restaurant and wandering the dock area of the marina late at night. He never spoke—and just as he'd done before to Chef Kevin—he would disappear in an instant upon being discovered.

No one can agree on who the specter may be. Some say it is the ghost of a local fisherman named Augustus Farley. He was lost at sea in 1879 when his ship vanished in a gale. Others are certain it is Old Man Eldridge hanging around, ensuring his marina and restaurant are being run properly. Either way, while the identity of the phantom fisherman remains a mystery, most folks here in Panama City seem to be okay with his presence.

Actually, whoever the phantom fisherman is, Chef Kevin says he's always welcome at Bayou Joe's.

Ghosts in the Spotlight!

The Martin Theatre stands dark and empty along Harrison Avenue in Panama City. The brightly colored panels of orange and blue across the front are fading, and plywood can be seen peeking through empty spaces that once held large plate-glass windows.

If you were to look at it today, you probably wouldn't believe that this building—once called the Ritz—was the most famous and beautiful theater in all of the South. Over the years, thousands of people came to see live theater, films, and concerts in the elegant surroundings. But everything would change on October 10, 2018, when Hurricane Michael took dead aim at Panama City. The Martin Theatre, like many of the buildings in town, was seriously damaged in the storm.

The hurricane may have destroyed the celebrated theater, but it could not scare away the many ghostly specters that call this theater home. It is not unusual for a theater to be haunted. Nearly every theater in the world, be it large or small, claims at least one in-house ghost. Panama City's Martin Theatre is no different. In fact, it seems to have more than its share of ghostly inhabitants, unexplained sounds, and even spine-chilling apparitions.

For many years, actors complained of shadowy figures lurking in the wings, as if waiting to go on stage. Gray-faced ladies in old-time clothing have been seen floating up the main staircase. Patrons who were happy to find themselves sitting next to an empty seat were sometimes shocked when a gray wispy figure joined them for the show. And, of course, there have been countless reports of odd footsteps, "unearthly" glowing lights, and cast members hearing their names called, despite nobody else being around. Some believe the theater might even have its own *ghost dog*, known for growling and running down the aisles before disappearing altogether.

But, as you can imagine by now, that's only half the story. The hauntings at the Martin Theatre didn't stop at ghosts in the attic and uninvited guests. Cast members have also complained of finding their costumes moved

about. It seems these backstage ghosts liked to "borrow" a single shoe from a costume, then leave it outside the director's door. Props were moved around, and sometimes the entire stage was re-arranged. As if remembering your lines isn't hard enough, ghosts taking charge of the props is the last thing any production needs!

Once, the crew raised the great curtain to the ceiling at the end of the night, only to find it mysteriously lowered the next morning. Another time, a photographer took a picture while in front of a dressing room mirror. Later, when the photographer looked at the image, she saw another figure standing directly behind her!

Though some actors and crew welcome visits from these ghostly spirits, others (even those who aren't quite sure they believe in all this ghostly business) refuse to be in the theater late at night. Even today, as the theater is being rebuilt, workmen complain of tools being misplaced and materials falling over. Sometimes, they hear the strange sound of someone mumbling or the pitter-patter of footsteps echoing off an empty stage.

Is the Martin Theatre really haunted? Are the ghostly shadows still lurking in the empty building? Are they waiting for the building to complete repairs so they can return to the stage and take a ghostly bow?

What do you think? The only way to *really* know is to come visit the Martin Theatre once the rebuild is complete. But here's some free advice: when you roll up to the concession stands, you might want to think of ordering treats for two, just in case.

The House Where No One Is Welcome

Lynn Haven took its name from a group of American Civil War veterans who fought for the Union and settled the town in 1911. Being such close neighbors, Lynn Haven and Panama City have many things in common, including their fair share of spooky places and haunted houses. One of these is an old house on Tennessee Avenue, which was built back in 1912.

The house has gone through many changes over the years. It has been repaired, repainted, and remodeled many times since it was first built. It has been rented by so many different people, the owner can't keep count. The tenants never grumbled about leaking pipes or chipped paint, but you can be sure that every single family that lived in the house complained about all the ghosts!

Some of you may have heard tales about haunted houses before, and some of you may have already made up your minds that no such place could ever exist, and that's all right. But for those who aren't so convinced yet, a word to the wise: be prepared, because just as a book cannot be judged by its cover, you can't tell if a house is haunted by merely looking at it. You may have a vision in your mind of a gravely decrepit mansion, now only a shadow of what it once was, standing on the top of a treacherous hill, with a backdrop of crashing thunder and lightning!

CUE THE CREEPY ORGAN MUSIC!

Well, that's the kind of haunted house you might see on Netflix or at the movie theater, but some believe that *real* haunted houses look just like all the other houses in the neighborhood. It could be an ultra-modern home with a lush garden. Or an apartment with a terrace overlooking the water. It could even be the house right next door, so keep your eyes peeled and stay alert. You never know . . . those neighbors of yours might just be ghosts!

Nearly everyone who has rented the home on Tennessee Avenue says they have heard footsteps running through the empty house. Apparently, this happens at all hours of the day and night, and the noise is so loud, it naturally wakes people from their sleep.

Others report that lights go off and on at

will, and sometimes the television channel is changed by invisible hands. In recent years, computers and cell phones will suddenly go dead, even when they are fully charged.

One resident had an unusual problem. If he left the windows open when he went out, every single window would be closed and locked when he returned. But if he shut all the windows before he left, the windows were wide open when he returned. It was so upsetting, he moved out after just two months.

Another tenant reported that one day he was having an argument with his brother, when orbs of light appeared from nowhere. They began to spin about the two brothers, moving faster and faster. When the brothers stopped to stare at the strange, swirling lights, a young girl with a long ponytail suddenly walked through the wall. She paused just for a moment and glared at them. Then she walked through the room and right out the front door, closing it behind her!

A few years later, a mother and her teenage daughter moved into the house. One Friday night, the girl went to a movie with her boyfriend. When they returned, he saw that her mother was sitting on a wicker chair on the side of the porch. He walked the girl to the door and said goodnight. As he drove away, he saw that the girl's mother had followed her inside. The next morning, he felt bad that he had not been very polite to the girl's mother. When he called to apologize, the girl started to laugh. She told him that he could not have seen her mother because her mom was not at home last night. In fact, she had been in a minor car accident in Pensacola and had spent the night in the hospital.

It wasn't much later when another family moved into the Tennessee Avenue home. While the parents were busy unpacking, their four-year-old son went upstairs to explore his new room. A few minutes later, he came charging down the stairs. His eyes were like saucers, and he was so excited that his words came tumbling out. He told his parents that the people who lived upstairs told him that this was their house and that they needed to get out. Later that day, the family smelled cigar smoke coming from that upstairs bedroom. They moved out soon afterward, too.

Not creepy enough for you?

There was one room in the house that no one wanted to sleep in. It was a downstairs bedroom that was always cold. People would shiver in their beds, even in the hottest Florida summer nights. One visitor said she felt the room was filled with a great sadness, and she even once saw a brown-haired woman hovering a few feet off the floor by the window! When she spoke to the spirit, it vanished into thin air.

So, you still don't believe in haunted houses. Well, wait until you hear about this completely paranormal phenomenon that occurs along the wall of one of the bedrooms inside the home on Tennessee Ave.

An old mirror in that same bedroom has been hanging there for as long as anyone can remember. Impossible as this may sound, oversized handprints appear on the mirror from out of nowhere. And although cleaning the mirror will wash them away for a time, they reappear soon afterward without explanation.

Well, no explanation that makes sense in this dimension, anyway! Because all bets are off when it comes to these haunted handprints. They don't belong to anyone who lives in the house, and no one knows why the prints continually appear on the old mirror.

Today, the house on Tennessee Avenue sits empty. A recent storm damaged it so severely, no one can live there. That is, no person *alive* could live there! But to a ghost, it could very well be a dream palace.

Ghostly Specter of the Schooner *Cleopatra*

Panama City's deep-water port has been one of the most important harbors in the entire Gulf Coast for more than two hundred years. And for at least that many years, the people living along St. Andrews Bay have shared tales of peculiar sightings, ghostly specters, and unexplained events.

That summer night, a boy named Cecil stood at his bedroom window staring out across the dock into the bay. It was after midnight and everyone was asleep. Well, everyone but Cecil. It was such a hot night that he couldn't get comfortable—there wasn't even a whisper of a breeze. Little did Cecil know, this would be a night he would never forget.

The bay was murky and still. It was too early for cargo ships to be moving about, and the fishing fleet had headed out to sea hours ago. The only light was the dim glow of a picture-perfect crescent moon.

At first, all Cecil saw was a grayish blur on the horizon. But then, as it moved closer, he could tell that it was a ship. It wasn't like any ship he had ever seen. It was a wooden two-masted schooner like they used over a hundred years ago. It appeared to be under full sail, its great white canvas billowing in an invisible wind.

As Cecil watched, the great ship seemed to float just above the water until it reached the dock. It sat there for a long time without moving. Despite the danger—and his disbelief—Cecil had to get a closer look. He crept out his window and crawled down the trellis to the ground, then darted across the yard to the dock.

He stood there for a while staring up at the strange wooden ship. There was no movement on board, and he couldn't see a single light. He walked alongside, searching for signs of life. He could see that the deck was crammed with dozens of barrels all held in place by a gigantic rope net. He stopped when he reached the rear of the ship and leaned sideways over the water to peek at the nameplate. It was hard to see in the dim light, but Cecil was able to make out the name. It was *Cleopatra*, just like the Egyptian queen.

After a while, Cecil decided to go home and get some sleep. He wanted to get up early to see the schooner in the daylight. But when he looked out his window the next morning, the ship was gone!

He rushed downstairs to tell his parents about what he had seen the night before.

"Oh, Cecil!" they said. "Such an imagination you have!" But when Cecil told them that the schooner's name was *Cleopatra*, his father's eyes popped open wide. He hurried to the bookcase and pulled out an old photo album from the shelf. Then, he began flipping through the pages until he came to the photo he wanted. He held the book out to Cecil. "Is this the ship you saw?" he asked.

Cecil jumped to his feet. "Yes, that's the one."

Before he could say more, his father said, "Son, you just saw a ghost. That was the schooner, *Cleopatra*. She was lost along with her two-man crew in a gale in 1902. She was loaded with over a hundred barrels of resin heading from St. Joe's to Pensacola." Cecil's father showed him the book. "See? Although she is gone, she sometimes makes an appearance right here, in her home port of St. Andrews Bay."

Cecil didn't say a word. He stared at the photo for a minute, then looked up at his father and smiled. He had seen a ghost, a *real* ghost: the misty apparition of the vessel known as the *Cleopatra*—lost at sea, but never in spirit.

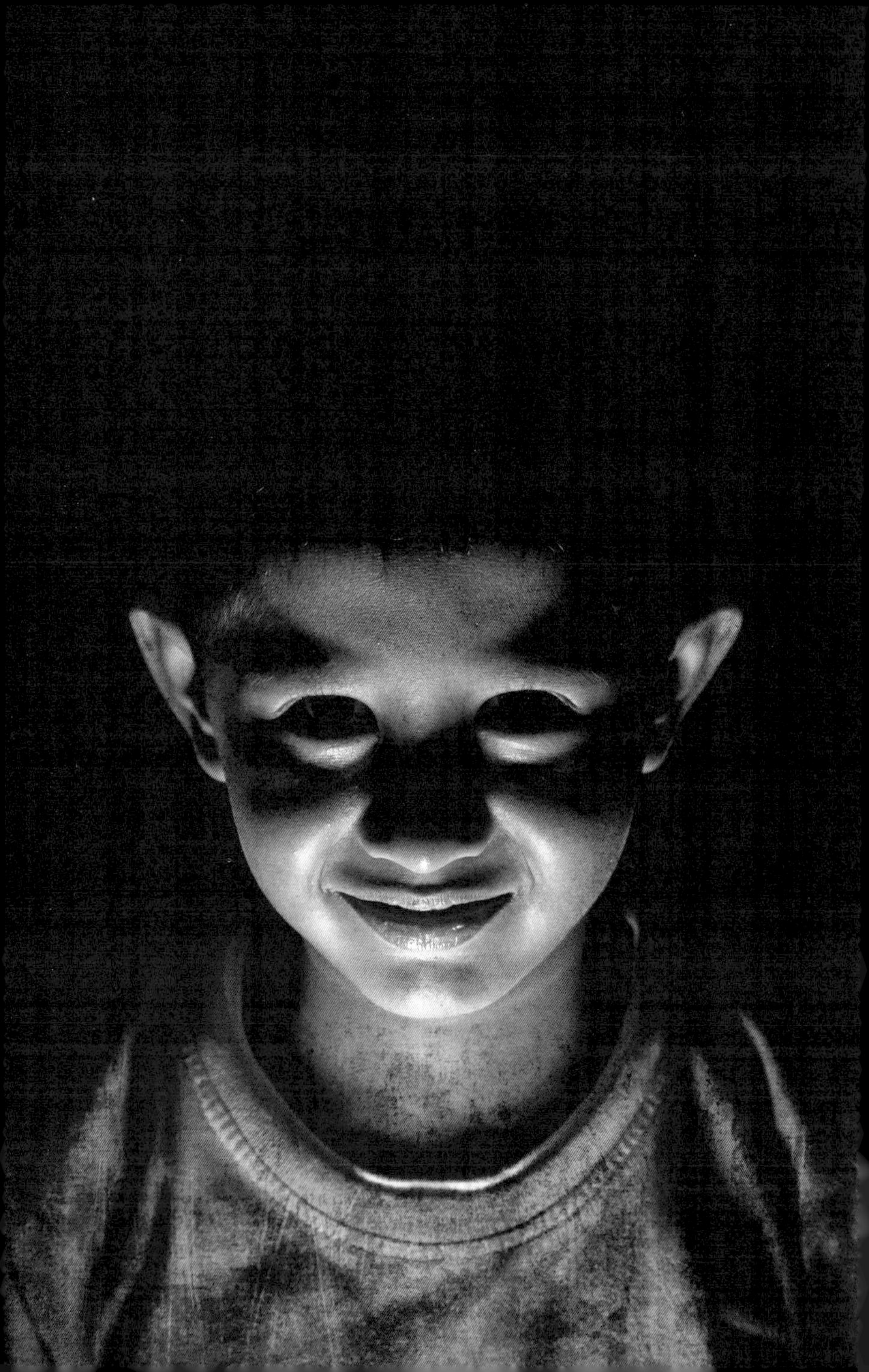

The Family That Adopted a Ghost

In most spooky tales, the ghost is either scary looking or behaves in a creepy or threatening manner. The humans who encounter the ghost are usually so frightened, they try to drive away the visiting spirit. But this tale of a haunting shared by a local Panama City family is very, very different. Not only was the family happy to have a ghost living with them, but the young teenage ghost was delighted to be adopted by a loving family!

It all started a few years ago when a young couple and their two sons, ages nine and twelve moved into their new house along Messalina Bayou. The cozy one-story house was their dream home. It was on a tree-lined street with a big yard and a dock with boat lift in the back. They thought it was a perfect home for their growing family. No one had a clue, of course, that the house was haunted.

The moving van had barely pulled away before spooky things began to happen. Moving

boxes toppled over, and furniture moved about by itself. No one paid too much attention to it at first. But by evening, they were also hearing unexplained sounds, like an occasional giggle, or the scratching of something unseen on the screen door.

The boys' mom thought her sons were playing jokes on her and gave it little thought. The next day, though, the strange activity continued. Lights went on and off, and the tv channel changed all by itself. She joked that perhaps the house was haunted, and they should keep an eye out for ghosts.

She should have kept her jokes to herself, it seems! That afternoon, while the boys were out exploring the neighborhood, their mom was sorting through the mountain of sporting gear they'd brought from the old house. She had already made two trips to the outside shed with deflated balls, old bats, knee pads, and fishing poles. Only two well-used boogie boards were left. She picked them up, tucked them under her right arm, and made one last trip to the shed.

She stepped into the shed and rested the boogie boards against the wall. But just as she turned to go, she saw him: a tall and skinny teenage boy, just a bit older than her own sons. He was wearing a dirty wet T-shirt and shorts. When she looked more closely, she could see a gush of dirty water falling from his clothes onto the shed floor. The boy's face was very pale, and his eyes reminded her of a lost child, scared and all alone. Instantly, a feeling of sadness filled the air. Shocked and confused, the woman backed out of the shed, took a deep breath to collect herself, then walked back inside to speak to the boy.

We do not know what she said, or if he was able to speak. What we *do* know is from that day forward, the family welcomed the ghost and treated him like a part of their family. This didn't mean he was always visible, or that he had stopped playing tricks on them. But the more they spoke with him, the more he seemed to hang around. Sometimes he could be seen, although usually just for a few seconds here and there. Other times, he would adjust the TV volume, turn on lights, strum the guitar, or tease guests by blowing on their hair. Whenever they had a backyard cookout, he loved to make their burger patties wiggle on their buns, or make the ketchup squirt out of the bottle in a great glob.

He was also known to put out the peanut butter for afternoon snacks, and he always made sure that he was included in family photos, appearing as a bright orb in the snapshot. However, it did seem to bother him when the children would fight. Sometimes when they were wrestling over a video game, the ghost would get their attention by tossing the game into the air, high over their heads.

Naturally, the family was curious about their adopted ghost. What had happened to him, and why he was still there? Although they searched for a long time, all they learned was that some years ago, a teenage boy had drowned in the Messalina Bayou, and that the cause of his death had been somewhat suspicious. The family often wondered if their adopted ghost was really the boy who drowned in the bayou. They never found out for sure, but for some unknown reason, it was clear he couldn't cross over to the other side. Perhaps he just liked them and didn't want to leave?

Or perhaps . . . he didn't even know he was dead.

Nonetheless, the friendly ghost is still there today—and still part of the family.

The Haunted Manor on Grace Avenue

Grace Avenue, in the heart of Panama City, was once a street filled with old and elegant single-family homes. The neighborhood was known for its well-kept houses with neatly trimmed lawns and gardens. Along the 900 block was a large white house with aqua shutters. It was sold many times over the years, and by the year 2000, the mysterious goings-on there were well known, as people began to call it the Haunted Manor. Residents and guests alike have reported hearing faraway voices, seeing shadowy figures walk right through the dining room walls, and feeling unusual bursts of cold air shooting throughout the first floor, as if an air conditioner was working full blast at all times. Once, it got so bad, a family was forced to regularly wear sweaters inside the house, regardless of the season! I'm sure by now I don't need to tell you they sold the house a short time later, but can you imagine living inside a ghostly igloo?

No thanks, I think I'll pass!

Not surprisingly, ghosts greeted the next owners immediately. The strange figure continued walking through walls; rooms filled with cigar smoke; and lights turned on and off without rhyme or reason. To make matters worse, every morning at 7:13, the cups and bowls flew from the pantry cabinets, crashing all across the kitchen floor. Motion detectors were installed throughout the house and were set off nearly every night.

Creeped out yet? Because it doesn't stop there: these ghosts held grudges, too!

For whatever reason, the ghosts did not seem to like Aaron, the new owner's teenage son. When Aaron told his father that he had seen a ghostly form hovering in an upstairs window, things got worse. Something began poking Arron in the back when he tried to sleep and even grabbed his feet and tried to tug him from the bed. Then one day, for no apparent reason, a sheet of window glass came loose from its frame and nearly hit Aaron as he was walking down the hall! The final straw came when Aaron climbed onto the porch roof to retrieve a lost ball. Someone, or *something*, gave him a shove, nearly knocking him off the roof!

Needless to say, the ghosts' "enthusiasm" at the haunted manor on Grace Avenue just hits a little differently than what you'd find at a typical haunted mansion...as typical as a haunted mansion can be! For whatever reason, these spirits *really* want the living to know they are here. They make noise, make surprise appearances, and sometimes make trouble—rearranging objects in the physical world so owners are stuck wondering what the heck is going on!

With the house having had so many different owners over the years, it makes sense some of them are eager to share their spooky experiences, while others want to forget the hauntings for as long as they live!

But this is just *one* of many haunted houses here in Panama City—not to mention, across all the United States. Chances are, you've walked right by one without even realizing it. (Maybe there's even one on your own street!) So, next time you're out for a stroll, take a look around your neighborhood—you may be surprised by what you find, hiding in plain sight!

A Ghost With a Mind of Its Own

One of the best-known buildings in the heart of Panama City is the Bay County Courthouse on East Fourth Street. It has been the home to county offices, courtrooms, and the county jail for more than one hundred years. It has also been home to many ghosts!

Back in the early 1900s, there was a rash of crime in the county. The sheriff and his deputies were kept busy tracking down cattle rustlers, horse thieves, and smugglers. The courts had a waiting list for trials, and the jail was overflowing. Bay County needed a new courthouse.

In 1915, the new courthouse was finished. People came from all over Florida to take part in the ribbon-cutting celebration opening the impressive new building. But just seven years later, disaster struck. A fire set by an inmate during an escape attempt filled the jail with flames and smoke. Although the

quick-thinking sheriff tried to put out the burning mattresses, there was a great deal of damage to the beautiful new building. No lives were lost in the fire, although it took several months to repair the damage.

Like other buildings in Panama City, the courthouse is no stranger to the unpredictable weather along the Gulf Coast. It has withstood floods, tornados, and countless tropical storms and hurricanes. Yet it is one of the best-known and most beautiful courthouses in all of Florida.

Rumors that the courthouse is haunted have been around for many years. Many of the strange events have been reported in the old basement area, an area off-limits to the public. Some staff refuse to go down to the lowest level of the basement because they say it is haunted. They have reported hearing sudden bursts of groaning that last for several minutes, only to stop just as suddenly as they started. In other areas of the courthouse, the feeling of being watched is a common complaint. Some have reported seeing a faceless female phantom who wanders near the courtroom wringing her hands and weeping. Other specters include a wispy female that seems happy to be there. She goes about her ghostly business seemingly unaware of anything going on around her.

However, one of the best-known hauntings in the courthouse may not be the work of a ghost at all. Ever since elevators were installed many years ago, one elevator seems to have a mind of its own. The haunted elevator will work properly for weeks at a time without a problem. Then, without warning, it plays a hair-raising trick on anyone who happens to be inside. When the haunted elevator is in this mood, passengers are in for the ride of a lifetime!

It doesn't matter which button you press or which floor you choose. Once you push a button, the elevator is in control. First, it zooms to the attic. Next, it stops with a jolt before suddenly plunging to the basement—then it repeats, on a nonstop loop! There is a short delay, and the door refuses to open. Then, finally—if you're lucky!—the elevator whisks you and the other passengers to the floor you requested. The elevator doors slide open, and the weak-in-the-knees riders rush out the door. It's no wonder at the Bay County courthouse, people often choose the stairs instead of the elevators!

How about you? Would you take the stairs? Or take your chances with an elevator that has a mind of its own?

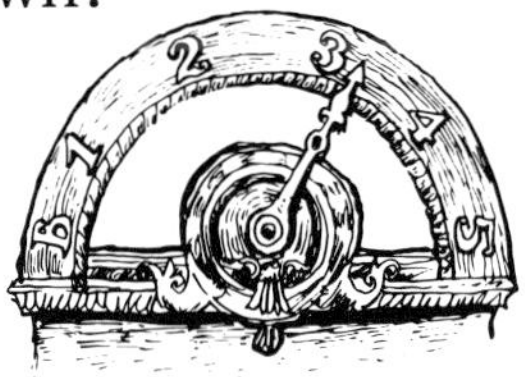

Ghostly Doubles Mean Double-Trouble

Many different kinds of ghosts can be found all across Panama City. There are spirits that can walk through walls, move things around, and even speak or make noises. Yet one unusual spirit is very different from all others.

As you know, ghosts are spirits of people or animals who are not alive. But this spirit is the opposite—it is a ghost of a person who is *still living*. You may have heard of this strange spirit;

it is called a ghostly twin or ghostly double. Its correct name is doppelganger. (Doppelganger is a German word made of two parts: "doppel," which means double or twin, and "ganger," which means walker.) So, a doppelganger is a kind of ghost that is an exact copy of a living person!

Although this kind of ghostly double is rare, people from all around the world have shared

stories about these unusual apparitions. Some believe it is bad luck to see this kind of other-worldly presence. They insist that if the ghostly double of a living person appears, danger will soon follow. In fact, it has been reported that President Abraham Lincoln saw his own ghostly twin on the morning of April 15, 1865. That evening, he was shot and killed at Ford Theater.

One morning at a law firm not far from City Hall, a lawyer asked his secretary, Megan, to put everything aside and work on an urgent report he needed for that very afternoon. The lawyer explained he had an important morning meeting and would stop back at the office at noon to pick up the report on his way to court. With one foot out the door, he called back, reminding Megan that it had to be ready by noon, and no later. Then, he was gone.

Megan worked slowly but carefully on the important papers. She knew there could not be any mistakes. When she was finished, she ran the spell checker to be sure it was perfect.

She smiled to herself as she glanced at her watch. It was only eleven o'clock, and the paper was ready. She placed the papers into a folder and carried it into her boss's office. But as she stepped through the door, she froze. There at his desk sat her boss. He was wearing the same dark blue suit he'd had on earlier and was staring at a dark computer screen. Megan was confused. She didn't know he had returned.

"I'm so sorry, I didn't hear you come in," she said. "Here's the file you need for court this afternoon." When her boss didn't answer, Megan placed the folder on his desk and returned to her workstation. It seemed strange that he had not spoken to her, but she figured he just had a lot on his mind.

It was just about noon when she happened to look out the window just in time to see her boss getting out of a taxi. Megan thought she was dreaming. Her boss was already in his office, so why was he getting out of a taxi? He had a car.

The back door swung open, and her boss rushed into the office shouting, "Are my files ready for court?"

Megan knew she had handed him the file an hour ago when he was sitting at his desk. She hadn't heard him leave, and now here he was, coming back through the door and asking for the file.

When she told him she had given him the folder at eleven o'clock, he looked puzzled and said, "Are you kidding? I wasn't here then. At eleven o'clock I was nearly wiped out by some guy who ran the red light on Harrison Avenue. He totaled my car!"

Megan followed him into his office, and there on the desk was the file, exactly where she'd put it earlier. She tried to explain what had happened, but he seemed to pay little attention. He scooped up his folders and headed for the door. He stopped for a minute

and said, "Megan, you better take the rest of the afternoon off; you need some rest."

That's when Megan realized what had happened: She had seen the ghostly twin of her boss! What she didn't know was if the auto accident would be his only misfortune . . . or if there was more trouble to come?

Haunted or Not? That Is the Question!

Of all the haunted places in Panama City, few are as well-known as the Martin House. The problem is that there are so many unusual stories about the old mansion that it is hard to know which ones to believe. These tales have been told and retold for more than one hundred years. They have been shared in newspapers, magazines, TV shows, and books. Almost everyone you meet in Panama City has heard at least *one* of the dozens of spooky tales about the house.

The Martin House was built in 1910 on the outskirts of town near Martin Lake. In its day, it was quite a grand house with a wide porch and windows on all sides to let in the sea breeze. It was spooky even then with the Spanish moss hanging from the branches of the tall oak trees on each side of the house.

Although a local legend says a murder took place inside the house, history has no record of the crime. But that doesn't keep people from repeating the story and claiming that it is the cause of all the strange and spooky things that have happened here.

The house was built on a large bit of land not far from a paper mill. It had several owners over the years, until 1932, when the paper company bought the building. It was used for meetings and special events for many years.

Today, the building sits abandoned and is not open to the public. A tall fence encircles the house with signs that read, "NO TRESPASSING" and "TRESPASSERS WILL BE PROSECUTED." Guards patrol the grounds around the house, and it is said that the paper mill has even installed electronic security devices to keep people away.

But this has not stopped those who need to see for themselves if the Martin House is as haunted as everyone says. Even today, there are new stories of the spine-chilling things that happen there.

It is not uncommon to see figures peering out the windows. Sometimes, these are large ghostly figures, and other times, they seem to be small children trying to get a look at the outside world. One sighting was of a lonely-looking little boy in old-time clothing holding a small teddy bear. Other ghost hunters have seen an angry-looking woman glaring through a window, and another a group of ghostly children playing on the porch. There have been other scary sightings, like the black-eyed ghost that haunts the second floor.

At the empty Martin House, those who come looking for ghosts usually find them. They hear footsteps, faraway voices, and the sound of soft weeping. One visitor claims to have heard a deep angry voice grunt, "Get out of my house!" Others describe seeing a bloodstain that never dries up. The terrifying sensation of being touched or poked by something unseen, as if an angry spirit wants them to leave. Chairs fly across the room, tables slide up against the wall, and a window shatters and then mysteriously repairs itself, over and over again.

Yet, despite all the paranormal proof, not everyone believes that the old Martin House is haunted. They say the old stories are just that—*stories* people tell to scare others away.

It is hard to know what to believe. Are the age-old tales of haunting true? Is something sinister *alive and well* inside these walls? Or... have the stories simply grown and flourished over the years, taking on a spooky life all their own? The truth is, we may never know for sure.

Why not visit this historic Panama City home and decide for yourself?

CHAPTER 10

The Lonely Ghost in the Window

When we look around St. Andrews Bay today, it is hard to imagine that one hundred and fifty years ago, the city wasn't a city at all. Not many people lived here. Those who did worked mostly in fishing, farming, or salt production. The seaport shipped cotton, local produce, and salt to ports all along the East Coast of the United States. The bay area was growing, and travelers had begun to gather here to enjoy the sandy beaches and cool ocean breezes. But everything changed when the Civil War began in 1861.

People went to work growing extra food and making war supplies for the Confederate Army. The cordial visits stopped, men were drafted into the army, and not long afterward, the Union used ships to block the Southern ports. This prevented locals from shipping war supplies, food, and salt to the Confederate Army.

Providing salt to the army was important because in those days, it was used to help preserve food. Without it, food spoiled before it reached the waiting troops. The South was determined to supply the troops, and the North was equally determined to prevent that.

On March 20, 1863, the Union ship, the *USS Roebuck*, entered St. Andrews Bay. It tried to land troops with plans to raid and destroy all local salt production. They were met by Southern soldiers, and there was a bloody clash. Soldiers were killed from both sides, and the Union was driven back to their ship.

On a bluff overlooking the struggle stood a three-story white clapboard house where you could see the entire bay from the front door. History doesn't tell us who owned it or what it may have been used for during the war. We only know that it sat next to a Confederate first aid station and was a witness to the fighting.

The house had several owners over the years. Then several decades ago, three women took over the building. They had a kitchen, pantry, dining room, and living room on the first level, and their bedrooms on the second. The third floor was a large single room with windows on four sides without curtains. The only furniture in the room was three chairs, three footstools, and three pillows. The women spent many hours here watching the bay. In the morning, they watched as the fishing boats headed out to sea, and in the evening, they sat in the semi-darkness watching as they returned. It was their favorite part of the house.

They ignored the strange noises they heard, saying that old houses always make strange sounds. No one said a word about hearing the *thud of heavy boots* on the stairs or the smell of tobacco that sometimes drifted down the stairwell. Whenever an icy breeze swept through the house on a hot August day, they smiled and were thankful for the cool air. They even laughed off comments from neighbors who insisted they sometimes saw a man in a uniform looking out the third-floor window.

One day, a neighborhood friend and her young daughter stopped in for tea. While the women chatted, the little girl played with a small doll with curly hair and a pink bonnet.

After a while, the girl got bored and wandered away from the table. With the doll in one hand, she began to climb the stairs, following the curved railing until she reached the very top floor.

She had only been upstairs a short time when the women heard the little girl giggling and talking to someone. They laughed to themselves, saying she must be talking to her doll. When it was time to go, her mother called her to come downstairs.

The little girl was laughing as she came down the stairs. Before anyone could say anything, she turned to the three ladies and asked if she could come over again and talk to the nice man in the blue "soldier suit" on the third floor.

When no one spoke, the little girl went on, saying that the man upstairs was a soldier, and he had to stay up there and keep watch. She said he told her funny stories, but he wished the war was over so he could go home to his family.

Her mother shook her head. "Oh, she's just pretending."

"No, I'm, not!" the little girl exclaimed. "I left my doll up there just to keep him company. So, can I come back tomorrow, please?"

Her mother grabbed her hand and took her home. The little girl never came back to visit her friend in the blue uniform, and the three old ladies who lived there didn't tell anyone about the little girl or her friend on the third floor. They did, however, keep the doll with the curly hair and pink bonnet, placing it on a little chair of its own, next to the window on the third floor.

Who or *what* was the phantom the young girl met on the third floor of the old house? Was it really a lonely spirit from the Civil War or just a figment of her imagination? Is it possible the ghostly solider is still there, haunting the old house to this day? Or has his soul moved on, reunited with his family at last? We may never know, but I'm sure the soldier would be happy to hear, thankfully, that the war did end.

Ghosts of the Cove

Today, the Cove is one of the best-known neighborhoods in Panama City. Located in the city's busy downtown, thousands of people live and work here. Like many places along the Gulf, the neighborhood has changed. For a long time, the Cove was mostly single-family homes. The narrow streets were lined with towering trees, each bending under the weight of the Spanish moss that hung off its branches.

This gave the Cove a spooky look any time of day.

It is an old part of town where some of the earliest houses were built. For hundreds of years, before the settlers from Europe arrived, the land belonged to the Chatot and Yucci Peoples. Today, their burial grounds lie beneath the streets of modern Panama City. So, it is not surprising that many of the hauntings here come from the fact that this was once their land and the final place of resting for many.

One long-time resident of the Cove, Carol, was not at all shocked when she realized that her house was haunted. After all, it was an old house; so old, no one knew exactly when it was built. The walls were crooked, and the floors were not level, but she didn't mind. She loved the house.

When Carol and her husband moved in,

they were surprised to find that the seller had left behind an old piano. Unsure what to do with it, they moved it out of the way to a little nook on the far side of the house.

The haunting began soon after they moved in. One night, Carol was sleeping when something woke her. She listened carefully. It was the sound of men talking. The voices sounded far away, yet Carol could tell it was in a language she had never heard before. After a few minutes, the voices died away. She fell back to sleep, and in the morning, she decided she had just been dreaming.

But then it happened again the next night. She listened with her ear up against the bedroom door. This time, she knew someone was in the house. She woke her husband and together they inched along the hallway, trying to hear what the men were saying. They had just reached the top of the staircase when the voices stopped. They searched the house, but there was no one there.

The next time that it happened, they were ready. The moment Carol heard the conversation, she woke her husband. He called the police and locked their door. When the police arrived, they found no one in the house except Carol and her husband, who had locked themselves in the bedroom. They also found all the doors and windows fastened, and the burglar alarm was still set. No one had entered the house.

By then, Carol was certain they had ghosts, and she knew it must be spirits from the Indigenous peoples who had once owned this land. She loved to read history, so she knew the Chatot and Yucci tribes had lived on this land for centuries. She suspected that her house was built on their sacred burial grounds. The nighty voices continued for so long that she became used to them and paid them little attention.

When spring came, Carol decided that she was tired of babysitting the old piano. Neither of them could play, and it took up too much space. She was pleased when a young musician answered her ad for a free piano. A few days later, he came with a few friends, and they heaved it into their truck and took it away.

Carol noticed right away that the house felt different. Once the piano was gone, they never again heard the voices. She can't say for sure if the ghostly voices were linked to the old piano, but the nighttime voices disappearing along with the piano is certainly an odd coincidence!

Not far from where Carol lives, there is a small cottage that was home to an old lady for many years. After she died, her niece Lisa moved into the house. Lisa was unpacking the moving boxes that morning when she suddenly felt someone hug her. There was no one else there, but she was certain she felt a hug. Although she was surprised by the embrace, she wasn't afraid. The air in the room felt warm and smelled sweet. The hugs began to happen more often. Soon, Lisa was looking forward to the loving hug each day. Then one day, just as she felt the invisible embrace begin, Lisa looked up. Standing next to her with her arms open wide was her aunt. Her bright blue eyes sparkled, although her face was nearly gray. Her flowing white gown seemed to flutter in the air. Before Lisa could speak, her aunt vanished.

This kind of ghost is often called a "crisis specter." This ghost is seen only one time, and it shows up when someone they loved needs help, is seriously ill, or is very sad. It appears only once and then vanishes. These unusual spirits are most often found at the scene of accidents, funerals, or when someone feels hopeless.

Some ghosts stay around because they have something they feel they must do. A spirit might be spotted where it once worked, trying to finish an important job, or it might stay with its family trying to make things better. Could that be why Lisa's aunt appeared before her in an instant? I guess anything is possible.

Lisa still lives in the little cottage in the Cove. We don't know if she still gets her daily hug from her departed aunt, but we sure like to think so.

A Haunting on Harrison Avenue

Everyone knows Harrison Avenue. It's the main street in the heart of Panama City and is home to government offices, stores, and restaurants. There are lots of interesting places to visit along the way. But one coral-colored building with aqua awnings on Harrison Avenue has a unique history and its own gathering of ghosts.

It has been home to many different businesses and stores since it was built in

1934. Back then, it was called Sherman Arcade. It had two large stores on the first floor and thirteen offices upstairs. At one time, there was a dentist, a beauty parlor, a lawyer, a shipping company, and an insurance company. The Girl Scouts once had an office here, too.

For as long as anyone can remember, there have been stories of ghost sightings, and claims that the building was haunted. The sound of footsteps were heard overhead, even when the building was empty. Many mentioned that they felt they were being watched and that they were never really alone in the building.

A few years ago, a local ghost hunter was walking through the building when she saw an old man sitting on the stairs. He was barefoot and wearing a pair of old farmers' jeans with a bib. The furrowed-faced man did not speak. He sat there with a faraway look on his face. A shadow seemed to be hanging over him and a feeling of great sadness was everywhere.

At one time, the studio for Panama City's TV station WMBB-TV was in this very building. The staff often remarked that they had a ghostly coworker. The sound of footsteps was often heard in the empty studio. File drawers would open and close by themselves, and batteries would go dead for no reason. Lights went on and off, and telephones would ring even when the wires were not connected.

Today, Millie's Café fills half of the bottom floor. People from all over the city drop into Millie's for many reasons. Some come for the New Orleans-style seafood, others for the great coffee and music, and some are looking for Millie, the house ghost.

It's believed that Millie, the ghost, is none other than the mother of the café's owner. She has been seen in the café, always wearing her favorite blue-and-white colored clothing. She's known to tease customers by touching them or to jolt the kitchen staff by moving spoons on the hanging rack.

The owner reported that one night after closing, he happened to look back into the restaurant and briefly saw a figure standing inside. When he went back to investigate, no one was there. He feels it was his mom checking out his café.

When Millie was alive, it was well-known that she loved her car more than anything else in the world. She kept it in perfect condition and even had her son wash and wax it every week. After she died, he sold the car.

The man who bought the car also lived in Panama City. One day shortly afterward, he drove it to the grocery store and went inside to shop. He had not been in the store long when he met an old friend.

"Is that your car in the parking lot?" he asked. When he said that it was, the friend looked surprised and then asked, "Who is that gray-haired old lady sitting in the driver's seat? She's clutching the steering wheel like she's doing a hundred miles an hour."

When they raced out to the parking lot, they found the car empty. But the owner knew that it was Millie's ghost sitting in the car because that is the way she always drove.

Wherever we happen to be in Panama City, we should keep an eye out for a ghost dressed in blue and white, because it just might be Millie.

Haunted Chairs & Ghostly in Pairs

In 1905, the area north of Panama City was covered by a dense forest. Many people worked in the lumber industry, while others grew vegetables on truck farms or fished from small boats in the local waters. When the land was sold to American Civil War Union veterans, everything changed.

They began arriving in 1911, and by 1912, houses went up all over the area. John Ackerson was one of the veterans who moved here, lured by the promise of warm weather, good soil, and the chance to become a landowner. Ackerson built a home on what is now Fourth Avenue, where he lived with his wife and children until he died in 1920.

A ghostly figure dressed in a blue Civil War Uniform was reportedly seen a few days after the death of John Ackerson. It floated up the main staircase and then seemed to inspect each and every room in the house. The spirit visited for a day or two and then disappeared, never to be seen again.

That may have been the home's first sign of ghostly activity, but it was certainly not the last! Before the settlers came, this land belonged to the local Indigenous tribes, the Chatot and Yucci. So, it is not a surprise that so many of the ghostly sightings around Panama City are those of unsettled spirits of Chatot and Yucci Peoples.

In 1930, word spread that the ghost of a Chatot woman dressed in traditional clothing and a feathered headdress had appeared in the kitchen of the Ackerson house. She stood with her hands on his hips, watching as the family cooked breakfast. In a few minutes, he vanished.

Years later, another family living in the old house claimed to hear muffled voices in upstairs bedrooms. When they entered the rooms, the voices disappeared. The same rooms had bursts of frigid air. More than once, clam shells or feathers were left behind.

Not so long ago, a couple who loved to go to garage sales moved into the house. At a local sale, they found what they thought was a real treasure. It was a pair of very old, unusual chairs. They later learned the carved wooden chairs had been made three hundred years ago, during the seventeenth century. Not only were they beautiful, but they were worth a great deal of money.

Although the couple brought the chairs home and placed them in the living room, no one was ever allowed to sit on them. When they grew tired of guarding the chairs from visitors, especially children, they moved the chairs to their bedroom.

One morning around dawn, the lady of the house awoke to find a man sitting in one of the chairs. She could not believe her eyes. The man was smartly dressed, although they were old-fashioned clothes. They stared at one another for what seemed like a long time. Just when it seemed that he was about to speak, the clock in the hall chimed and the man vanished. The woman and her husband were so afraid that the chairs were haunted, they locked them in a storage room. They sold the chairs soon afterward.

Did the ghost of John Ackerson return to make sure his house was in order? Is the ghostly woman in the kitchen still waiting for her breakfast? And . . . can a chair really be haunted?

Can a Lighthouse Outrun Its Ghosts?

Cape San Blas juts out into the Gulf of Mexico from the mainland near the port of St. Joe. Built in 1849, the lighthouse guided thousands of ships through the shallow waters found in this part of the Gulf for more than a hundred and fifty years. Without it, ships could not pass safely around the cape. The lighthouse faced many problems because of its location. It was at the mercy of ocean storms, hurricanes, and erosion (the constant wearing away of the shoreline).

A new brick lighthouse had to be built in 1851 because a storm had destroyed the first one. But five years later, the water had reached within eight feet of the door of the new light. Protecting the lighthouse from the Gulf of Mexico was becoming a full-time job.

In 1883, a new ninety-eight-foot metal lighthouse was built farther back from the water. It was made of eight huge cast iron legs, with a watchtower and lantern at the top. A spiral staircase ran up the center. But Mother Nature still had other plans. Storms and ongoing erosion forced the lighthouse to be moved farther inland once again.

Something had to be done. In 2014, the lighthouse on Cape San Blas was taken apart and loaded into trucks. The keeper's house and oil shed were packed onto wide load carriers. A

long convoy of trucks and carriers moved the massive tower and the two buildings fourteen miles to the park in St Joe's. It took nearly two days to make the move with thousands watching along the way.

The lighthouse was put back together and then set on a cement base. The keeper's house and the oil shed were then attached to new brick foundations to hold them in place. Within a few days, things were back to normal. The lighthouse beam stretched fourteen miles into the Gulf, once again lighting the way for ships.

Today, the lighthouse rests in St. Joe's at George Core Park, also known as Lighthouse Park. Thousands visit each year, eager to climb the tower and look out over the beautiful white sand beaches.

Workers at the gift shop insist that they have not had any ghostly experiences since the lighthouse moved to St Joe's. But they do admit that people often ask if the lighthouse is haunted.

This might seem a bit strange. When the lighthouse was on the shoreline of Cape San Blas, there were many reports of hauntings and unexplained events. According to local tales, a lighthouse keeper died on duty in 1932. Some say his was a violent death, while others say he died due to hard work and the loneliness of the keeper's job. Others say he died of a broken heart. We will never know.

Soon afterward, there were reports that the old keeper's ghost appeared near the base of the lighthouse whenever bad weather approached. Some claimed to see him climbing the stairs to make certain that the lantern was lit. For some time, people stayed away from the lighthouse because of the feeling of sadness in the air.

Then, just six years later in 1938, the new

lighthouse keeper was murdered. From then on, the area around the base of the lighthouse always felt cold, even in hot weather. Some said that his spirit roamed the grounds looking for his killer.

In the 1950s, a tragic accident at the lighthouse took two more lives. Workers were painting the lighthouse when their safety rope broke. The two men fell to their deaths. Ever since, there have been reports of grayish figures painting the lighthouse in the moonlight. Spookier still, near the anniversary of their deaths, people claimed to hear the sound of piercing screams.

As time goes by, fewer stories are told about the ghosts of the lighthouse. Workers at Lighthouse Park have not reported any ghostly sightings since the move. Perhaps these restless spirits have faded away. Or, could it be that the lighthouse at St. Joe's has outrun its ghosts?

A Ghostly Goodbye

Now that we've told you all there is to know about the ghostly dealings and demonic dwellings in Panama City, how do you feel about the existence of ghosts *now*? Still unsure?

The only way to find out for certain would be to visit the remains of the Martin Theater and see if anything gets you to jump from what is still left of your seat.

No matter what happens, the menu at Bayou Joe's is too much to resist to worry about a haunting from the great beyond during dinner.

Panama City has so much beauty to offer, who could resist a walk along the shores of St. Andrews Bay at sunset? Just keep in mind that if a schooner arrives from nowhere and the captain offers you a ride, ask him what year he was born before hopping onboard—just to make sure he's of this century—and this universe!

Patricia Heyer is a local history buff with a special interest in New Jersey folklore and marine science. She has written extensively for both children and adults during her career. Her most recent title, *The Ghostly Tales of the Jersey Shore,* was released in 2023. Pat is an avid reader, beachcomber, and animal rescue supporter. She resides on the Jersey shore with her husband Rob and their rescue cat, Gracie. You can learn more at: www.heyerwriter.com

Check out some of the other *Spooky America* titles available now!

Spooky America was adapted from the creeptastic *Haunted America* series for adults. *Haunted America* explores historical haunts in cities and regions across America. Here's more from the original *Haunted Panama City* author, Beverly Nield:

www.ancestry-pi.com